Autumn

Nicola Baxter

Illustrated by Kim Woolley

 CHILDRENS PRESS ®

A Division of Grolier Publishing
New York ● London ● Hong Kong ● Sydney
Danbury, Connecticut

2866531

Summer is the warmest time of the year.
The sun shines and you can play outdoors.
Gradually, the weather grows cooler again.
Autumn is coming.

Now try this...
How can you tell that the next picture shows an
autumn scene?

3

In the early days of autumn,
fruits and seeds ripen on the trees.
There is plenty for birds and animals to eat.

Now try this...
Do you recognize these fruits and seeds?
Which ones can people eat?

But winter is coming.
Birds and animals need to eat a lot now.
Soon it will be hard to find food.
Some animals will store their
food for winter.

As the weather gets colder,
some animals find a warm
nest, burrow, or cave
to sleep in.

This is called hibernating.
They do not wake
up until spring!

Some birds and animals move
to warmer places
when the weather gets colder.
Birds and insects may fly
thousands of miles.
In the spring, they fly back again!

Try this later...
Moving to another place is called migrating.
Find out which animals and birds migrate to or
from your area.

Some trees are evergreen.
They keep their leaves all winter.
But on many trees, the leaves begin to die

Try this later...
Autumn leaves turn beautiful colors.
Collect some of the prettiest ones.
Glue them on construction paper
to make an autumn picture.

Autumn winds blow the leaves
from the trees.
Soon the branches are bare.

15

On some autumn mornings,
it is misty, making it
hard to see very far ahead!

Sometimes a frost overnight
makes everything sparkle.

Gradually during the autumn,
the days become shorter.
It gets dark quite early in the evening.

Try this later...

On cold, dark evenings, it is warm inside.
What do you do when you come home from school?

19

In the middle of autumn,
Halloween makes scary things fun.

Try this later...
Ask a grown-up to help you
carve a pumpkin and make
a jack-o'-lantern.

20

As the autumn passes, the days become colder and colder until... winter is here.

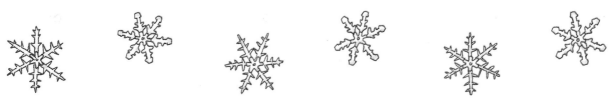

Index

© 1996 Franklin Watts

First American Edition © 1996 by
Children's Press
A Division of Grolier Publishing
Sherman Turnpike
Danbury, Connecticut 06816

Library of Congress Cataloging-in-
Publication Data
    Autumn / Nicola Baxter.
      p. cm. — (Toppers)
    Includes index.
    Summary: A simple discussion
of various facets of autumn,
including animal hibernation and
migration, leaves changing colors
and falling, and the Halloween
holiday.
    ISBN 0-516-09276-6
    1. Autumn—Juvenile literature.
[1. Autumn.] I. Title. II Series: Baxter,
Nicola. Toppers.
QB637.7.B39 1996   95-50047
508—dc20   CIP AC

Editor: Sarah Ridley
Designer: Kirstie Billingham
Picture researcher: Sarah Moule

Acknowledgements: the publishers
would like to thank Carol Olivier and
Kenmont Primary School for their help
with the cover for this book.

Photographs: Bruce Coleman Ltd 11;
James Davis Travel Photography 13;
Robert Harding Picture Library 14, 17;
Peter Millard cover; NHPA 5, 7, 23;
Oxford Scientific Films/Animals
Animals 9; Trip 3; ZEFA 16, 21.